Praise

Bill Newby's *Passing Through* delights, surprises, teaches, and sings poems with knowledge and wisdom. Most impressive is the collection's combination of a multitude of subjects—from baseball to Cambodia, from "how to hold a pencil" to George Floyd-- mixed with a command of craft in image and music, metaphor and pacing. No matter the subject, most impressive about the poems, as in all satisfying poetry, is Newby's skills at merging detail with metaphor and music. *Passing Through* is an ambitious museum you'll want not only to pass through, but "pause"... and linger over this deeply satisfying—and humane—gallery of poems.

Philip Terman - Author of *This Crazy Devotion*
Former Director, Chautauqua Writers Festival

Bill Newby's second collection, *Passing Through*, offers readers much-needed moments of pause and pockets of time to slow down and relish in the crafted language and resonant imagery of his poems. Wry and wise, his companionable voice invites us to enter these spacious rooms, to sidle up alongside him, to live and observe our lives more fully.

David Hassler – Author of *Red Kimono, Yellow Barn*
Director, Wick Poetry Center, Kent State University

"Pick it up with gratitude." This sage instruction from Bill Newby's poem "How to Hold a Pencil" is equally applicable to his welcome second collection *Passing Through*. In poems of observation and lamentation, Newby shares a wry sense of humor, companionable wit, and deep sense of empathy. From globetrotting adventures abroad to a masked and gloved expedition to the grocery store amid our global pandemic, Newby invites us to ride shotgun through his passages to destinations near and far, and into his memories of experiences never to be had again. These are trips well worth taking.

Jonathan Haupt – Director, Pat Conroy Literary Center

PASSING THROUGH

Poems by

Bill Newby

for Makael

ACKNOWLEDGEMENTS

Thanks to the editors of the following
where some of these poems first appeared,
sometimes in slightly different form.

Blue Mountain Review: Going to O'Hare in Fog

Bluffton Breeze: Drenched Again

Ebb & Flow (Island Writers' Network):   Security Questions

Fish Tales Poetry Contest
(Palm Beach Poetry Festival):   Hooked

Ohio Teachers Write: Sweater-Scented

Reflections (Island Writers' Network):   Hole-in-One Club
                                             Holiday Herds

Sixfold: Clean Pants
                                             First Ladies at Ruby Lee's
                                             Photography 201: Selfies
                                             Sending a Kiss from Third
                                             Touring

Time & Tide (Island Writers' Network): Angkor Wat

CONTENTS

Performance Relocated

Touring

Eight Minutes and Forty-Six Seconds

Passing Through

Robin in Fog

University Still Life

Yesterday's Oars

Performance Relocated

Hole-in-One Club

I'm still waiting for my magic shot.

Every other week someone else's name
graces the pro shop's door,
and we're invited to get our free drink
over the next two weeks—
a chance to join the celebration
and schmooze with the current star
whose been given license to strut and gloat.

Joy comes to some of us in more modest attire,
like finding the fairway or landing near the green.

So we practice and practice,
place another and another ball on the ground or tee,
while muttering mantras like "stay in the shot"

And swing by swing we try to chisel a groove
into our hands and arms, torso and thighs—
a groove we hope to easily revisit,
like the way our fingers tie a shoelace
and our hands draw a razor across our cheek.

But for many of us, our bodies are forgetful,
and like traveling without directions
we amble from stop sign to stop sign,
making stab after stab, hoping for the best.

So, in those rare moments when anyone, anyone,
hits from the tee box and drops that two-inch ball
into that four-inch hole,
it feels as miraculous as water changing into wine,
or at least a beer or mixed drink at the bar.

Target Practice

Is there any hope?
Will man ever improve?

Up and down each interstate,
in each rest area
and at every wind swept truck stop,
I reflect on our progress.

The cathedrals of Europe,
the Egyptian pyramids,
the Great Wall of China.
Every stone required precision.
Each had to be laid
in an exact spot.

Bands of hunters left their caves
in pale morning light,
and their ability to locate and slice a jugular
separated survivors from has-beens.

In techno-numbed faith
we pack ourselves
into aisle, middle, and window seats,
trusting that our pilot can gently return us
to the center line
of a lengthy runway.

And for generations we've practiced,
hour by hour, day by day.
Pouring coffee into a cup,
reaching for a door handle,

squaring a stamp in the top right corner,
putting toothpaste on a brush.

It makes one wonder
why so many men
miss the urinal.

New Monday Hours

Even during the new, longer Spring Break hours,
on Monday mornings the outlets are dead.

There's only one salesperson in each shop,
and they aren't visible from the front window.

Only when the doorbell rings
do they appear from the stockroom
and offer a clear-eyed, smiling welcome.

No one is rushing or tapping steering wheel fingers
as shrunken drivers in oversized SUV's
inch out of the sole space near the end of an aisle.

Sidewalk rockers anchor no butt or kick.
Trash cans are empty,
and the rocket ride quietly waits
for its breakfast quarters.

Starbucks' baristas have plenty of time
to discuss their husbands' latest gaffs
and what it was like before the mall opened.

And the restrooms remain clean all day.

A Premium Blend

Like a fine tea,
she brewed her life
with special care,

steeping laughter and wisdom,
guidance and play
into everyone's cup.

And in her final moments,
when she could no longer pour,
we gathered at her bedside

and shared sips of the many treasures
we carry with us
and will continue to savor

as long as we live.

Back Porch Meditation

Silence. Quiet.
Time to listen, listen, listen.

Each day the same.
Each day different.
Another breath.
Another death.

Quiet. Calm.

Wait. Watch. Wonder.
Listen. Allow. Be.

The symphony plays on.
The stage lighting shifts.
Players enter, perform and leave.
Wasps build. Anoles scamper.
The sun slowly moves around each post.

Here. Now.
Here. Now.

Sending a Kiss from Third

Every infield is different.
The ground may be as smooth as tarmac
or loose as a hiking trail –
groomed like the Masters
or as shaggy and snarled as the Turner's tree lawn.

But the only way to play
is with hope for a true bounce
and prayer to snatch a liar.

The game is slow
with lots of room to itch and scratch, spit and stare,
but the window for strolling and shifting shuts
when the ball leaves the pitcher's hand.

Then it's time for low, ready balance –
each foot dug in, hugging the earth,
and arms long and loose before bent knees,
like willow branches nearing the ground.

But as low as you get, your head must be up,
as if you've crept close in a tiger crouch
with your muscles loaded and ready to pounce.

And in these key seconds the world must disappear,
for the only story's at the plate
where you need to read
the back and arms' unwinding torque
as the bat flows in a wide circle
and greets the ball with a crack or ping,
that darts like a bullet aimed at your head

or skitters like a stone skipping water,
seeking a pebble or divot that might shift its course.

This is what you've trained for
and why you've oiled your glove,
pounded a predictable pocket
and even taken dance lessons.

In this instant, the only time is **now**.
Now you must welcome its flight,
delight in its arrival,
and reach wide or close, low or high,
to draw it into your mitt,
embrace it with your free fingers,
and hug and grasp it as you slide toward first,
skating left while loading right,
loading your arm like a jitterbug back step
before pulling your partner into another twirl,
gripping the ball like a door knob
before flinging it wide open.

Then whip your arm, free and relaxed,
free and flowing across your body,
as you turn around your spine
and look at the first baseman's mitt,
like a lover's face arced up and begging for a kiss,
as you let the ball go.

Stuck

Indecision grabs me at each hurdle.
It wraps my brain in a blanket of doubt
and leaves me uncertain of the next best step.

Do I understand enough
about this ice's crystalline structure?

How slippery the slope?
How quickly it could break?
What's lurking below?

Every near period morphs into a question mark,
and yesterday's mail becomes tomorrow's pile.

My lists grow. The stack climbs.

The lock around my time
gets harder and harder to pick.

Thirteen Views of Racquetball

1   diet Pepsi?
     no thanks! regular

2   that voice
     that smile
     old stories
     the latest news

3   draw the curtain
     think of your game
     only your game

4   an island of blue
     no papers, no troubles
     a spot in space
     a spot in mind

5   patience within awareness
     awareness within movement
     time extends
     the doorway opens
     let ki flow through it

6   athletic Rorschach
     assertive or passive
     straight-forward or crafty
     brawn or brains

     ah yes, this type again

7   wristlet soaked, brow beaded
    droplets on the floor
    shoes sliding and heart pounding
    short of breath
    pushing, pushing, pushing

8   one ball
    two players
    six walls
    two lines
    seven shots

    infinite permutations in a finite world

9   shape-altering compression
    storing energy
    spontaneously discharged
    in an explosive return to form

    distortion
    normality
    distortion
    normality

10 within Picasso's nightmare
    a cubist playground
    on display for wandering critics

11 being the pin within the pinball
    working the flippers

    watching the game within the game
    flashing scoreboards within your head

kicking in another ball
before the quarter runs out

12 ego hyped
ego squashed
elation and despair

an emotional elevator
stopping at unpredictable floors

13 momentary immortality
will denying age
sprinting to obscure the slowing clock

Ball Control

At dinner we seem in uneven teams
of talkers and listeners.

Some grab the ball and dribble
all over the table.

Everyone else plays zone.
They watch, listen, sit and smile.

Even the waiter has to wait,
standing a bit off court,

hoping to find a break
between first love and career.

But the ball remains in the talkers' court
and rarely is tossed to the other team.

Small Town Mysteries

Highway workmen in torn jeans,
boots, orange vests and sweat
flip STOP and SLOW signs,
then wave us across the gravel,
around cement trucks and tractors,

while we juggle town maps
framed by ads for hair styling,
sandals, golf and dinners
and try to find street signs in the mid-day glare
along the corridor of Swiss-dressed inns
on our way to Main Street.

It's like opening another work by a favorite novelist.
New names populate a familiar landscape.
It's a tourist town with pockets of local wealth,
a grey stone bank at the corner of 1st,
and a series of curio shops dancing
between clever, cute, traditional and exotic.

We pause at realtors' picture windows
to inhale the scent of properties in the oven –
a cabin and broad front porch in the woods,
a brick Georgian with white columns and a circle drive,
and a simple two-story clapboard by a lake.

It's easy to imagine moving in.
The swept sidewalks, roadside benches,
and evenly spaced pots of flowers by the curb
make everything feel idyllic.

Like every teenager would be acne-free,
and every doctor would have time to talk.

But we know first impressions can be misleading
and that later chapters often rip away the veneer
hiding the ugly underbelly
behind such pastel settings.

Mid-August Friday Morning

The world quiets when schools open.
A few northerners are still vacationing
and pedaling their way to the beach
like the long underbelly of a parading Chinese dragon.

But classrooms have gobbled
the morning porch shouts,
the pre-teen fights around the pool,
and the shore-side chatter
while trying to throw the minnow net
in a wide circling toss.

Lawn crews' saxophones take turns
on riffs of leaf blowing,
but the screeching violins and impatient trumpets
have been bussed to another stage.

Drenched Again

Early August morning rains
draw a silver sheet across the lagoon.

Fierce as a drummer's solo,
roof water attacks the railing,

bursts like July 4th sparklers,
and settles in a deck mirror.

Afterward, the platinum sky is flawless.
No nick or smudge mars its smooth surface

spread bright behind stands of dark pines
like clumps of lint caught in feather dusters.

No fish jumps. No ripples sweep.
Minnows lounge in the grasses.

Bikers' Mutiny

At the apron of every cart path leaving the road,
bolted to a sturdy, square, four-by-four post,
there's a large wooden sign with a black background
and a block-lettered white message:

NO WALKING OR BIKING

Though the message is clear,
the sign seems unbalanced.

And closer examination shows we don't need
an Egyptologist to decipher hieroglyphics
or a team of summer archeologists
to grid, trowel, brush and sift.
We have enough remaining evidence
to build our own story.

Despite the layers of black paint,
from the dark, grainy background
where a router once birthed them,
like a community of the undead
rising from their midnight graves,
anyone can see the cloaked qualifiers:

7 AM – 7 PM

These skeletal characters show
what they tried to bury:
that years ago a developer used
cart paths to market lots.

It's an ironic sign —
promoting what it's trying to halt.

Instead of choking enthusiasm,
it reminds all comers
of yesterday's pleasures
and today's opportunity
to ignore the rules.

Just like how a dessert's extra sprinkles
or a woman's bright smile
can break a diet or challenge one's fidelity,
the chance to cycle away from cars,
in and around the open light
of fairways and greens,
lakes, ponds and streams,
is so compelling that every evening
groups of bikers sing and laugh
speeding past these signs
and often pause at the bridge
to take photos memorializing
their defiant delight.

Hooked

The point dents
     a dimple
     then a furrow
     then a pit
breaking fast-as-water
diving into hidden guts.

With the firmness of a contract
whose clauses are binding
and where penalties fall fast and hard,
the blade slides forward
     flesh hugging the bevel
     caressing its cold symmetry
     then gracefully parting
     in a flange of speckled mucus.

    My guts tighten.
    My eyelids zip.

    No splitting, spitting sickness
    is wanted now.

And the knife saws gritting
through the bone.

Performance Relocated

We sit quietly, look and wait.
Like getting early to a concert,
we wonder when the players will arrive.

After all the advertising –
the headlines, updates and flood warnings –
the overhead grey and driveway dry spot
feel disappointing.

We purchased great seats
by broad picture windows
high over the lowered lagoon.

But the orchestra appears headed
for a far off northern hall,
so we might need to give it up,
find our car,
and head for a movie.

On Clauer's Back Porch

As the warm November sun
threads through the pines

and mariachi melodies
leap across the fence line,

the calm quiet of Thanksgiving Day
reaches its arms around us

and, like an approaching island
in an ocean of labors, whispers,

"Here you can rest."

Lake Erie, Near Euclid Creek

It's over a mile
before the water turns from grey to blue
and sits like a bead of welting
running beneath the horizon.

The rest lays flat
like a firm cushion along the break walls
waiting for us to lie across the slow swells.

Birds chirp high in the trees
while scores of others dive and dart
from shadow to sunlight,
filling every opening.

A cool Canadian breeze
freshens the southern shore.

Silenced

Bob Masteller (1938 – 2015)

The trumpet stands at ease.
The mute is in our ears.

In the middle of the night
a car pauses at the top of the bridge
and is found there in the morning.

No shirt, no shoes, no sweats, no note.
Just a 32 POINT HEADLINE
and silence at dawn.

The lights are off.
The door is locked,
and love lingers on everyone's lips.

Every melody ends.
Every player takes his part,
croons, crows, chugs and chats,
then steps aside.

We talk, we wait, and we wonder
when we'll be ready to sing again.

Touring

Leaving Home

We travel in anxiety and return in comfort.

We pack clothes and meds for all occasions
and drag our insecurities

through airports and train stations,
up escalators and over cobble stones and gravel

in search of the other as long as it doesn't infect
and rush us to the nearest toilet or drug store

where we can't read the packages
or talk our way to certainty.

Foreign comes in a colorful wrapper
we want to see and touch

but are often afraid to swallow.

"Turkish Automobile Association"
(Backseat Observations
Traveling through Turkey)

TAA reps are everywhere –
walking near the lettuce field ditch,
standing at crosswalks waiting for the light,
pumping gas in the next aisle.

Some are experts and can describe
the stand of praying trees, crippled house,
wavering waterfall or bridge
at each key turn for the next fifty kilometers.

Others wish they could help
but are also far from home,
or someone else takes them
when they need to go.

Guides may also disagree –
what comes through the left window
may not square with offerings on the right.

And your own memory shelves
may collapse in clutter
and leave nothing clear
but the reach of the open road.

Every approach has its costs.

GPS creates false self-confidence
through a tiny screen that never connects
ear and foot, tail and tusk.

Paper maps rip, fall out of date,
and can be as bewildering as Sunday's crossword.

And roadside stops are as unreliable as gossip
and may be knotted like windblown hair.

But TAA travelers can hear the local dialect,
snack on stories and dump complaints
every step of the way.

Angkor Wat

We walk the ruins watching our steps
and the dancers frozen in stone
holding their pose and youth,
celebrating lives surrounded by dragons,
seven headed snakes,
and thousands of soldiers, craftsmen and judges
protecting the nation and issuing eternal punishments
for temporal indiscretions.

Invaders emptied the cities
and the jungle overran the temples
while wind and rain stripped the stucco's Kodachrome
and left a sepia field in its place.

Through the king's gate
we climb steps toward the heavens
and hardly pause where priests sat silent
hour after hour, seeking blessings.

But we stop only long enough
to digitize a moment
we hope will inspire us back home.

Touring

We step off the bus
lugging the Ten Commandments
and the accumulated weight
of western civilization's struggle with brotherly love
tucked in our backpack
next to another plastic bottle
of cool, filtered, spring water.

Our Lowe, REI, and Merrell boots
provide arch support for our modern egos
and protect our feet from the dust, stones and debris
still lingering from Pol Pot's house cleaning.

Far beyond the moat,
backlit across the skyline of harsh mid-morning glare
lays the silent silhouette of Angkor Wat,
small, black, symmetrical lotus bulbs
cut free from the jungle
to provide power for a tourist economy
annually outpacing last year's records.

Shaven, saffron draped, Buddhist monks
move wordlessly in the shadow of a neighboring pagoda
while we make electronic records of ornate stupas

then pause at the southern entrance for a group photo
before joining the flow of sweltering gawkers
walking the surrounding corridors

where thousands of patient artisans
chiseled stone reminders of the painful damnations
born of infidelity.

The actors wear different masks –
snakes, dragons, phoenixes and turtles,
farmers, fishermen, servants and soldiers –
but the plot is as common as yesterday's *Times*.

Our shirts cling and sweat oozes across our cheeks,
but our air-conditioned bus is nearby,
and we can wash before lunch.

Cosmetics

"Rice fields are books. Hoes are pencils."
Khmer Rouge Motto

The doorway to the purge opened with disguise.
Crowds lined the streets, cheered and danced,
welcoming their liberators
who had come to protect them.

It's an age old story –
a Trojan horse with a viperous belly,
smallpox blankets for the natives,
Big Macs that weaken our knees.

And as Odysseus learned
returning home can take years of challenge,
especially when all priests and teachers,
scientists and civil servants
have been eliminated.

The lock on power opens slowly –
twelve steps, twelve years,
that feel like twelve generations.

But at last it's time
to get wholesome hands back on the wheel,
build roads and bridges, paint and post signs,
and pick paths of better purpose
without forgetting history's warnings
along the way.

Mid-Day Mekong

Like a liquid conveyor belt,
the tide moves life between hull and shore.

Clumps of water hyacinth bob
like supplicants at prayer,
their green palms reach skyward
as they wait for a crossing rudder
to lift them to a better channel.

Sampans with sun-bleached prows
and empty fishing nets draped over stern railings
chug upstream ahead of long-shafted propellers.

Broad-nosed barges pass with red motorbikes
laying on black tarps that hide mountains of cargo
while a nonstop radiator stream
pisses off the back deck.

Shirtless men in high canvas chairs
lean back, smoke and toe-turn their tillers
while women squat behind
on boards stretching over the water
as they dip, squeeze, and caress clothes
lifted in and out of scarred plastic pails.

A light tower sits silently above an island's edge.
A rooster crows from a hidden yard.
A floating derrick waits for the next empty barge.

Like a steam iron on high,
heat presses the day.

The Untold

We were riding in the knowledge bus,
looking, listening, asking, probing,

taking notes, etching synapses,
comparing ours to theirs.

We had the best – men of character, striving,
good humor, fluent English, and lots of information.

And kilometer by kilometer, they stacked our brains
with reams of history, customs and data.

But in every story, there are hidden parts,
things no guide would tell.

What market merchants say to each other
after telling tourists they bargained well.

The sound of rain on plastic sheeting
in the fifth flood week away from home.

The half-life of inner peace
as you get further from the temple.

When street food becomes delightful
and the fear of chills and diarrhea leaves.

How long it might take for citizens
to care about the garbage.

Which is better? A serving of world news,

or another walk through the village.

What monks say to each other
when sharing the same motorbike.

What parents tell children
about sautéed worms and fried crickets.

The feeling of tied, leather shoes
after a full life of flip-flops.

When arranged becomes arousing,
and one goes to bed with comfort and desire.

Strolling Saigon

We hide our wallets and carry
water bottles and a spacious microchip,
seeking adventure amid the pickpockets,
shysters, and everyday folk.

At every corner, down every alley,
in dark doorways and on filigreed balconies,
like the faces of a fresh deck of cards,
the common and unusual thumb past.

Men gather on sidewalks
in the shade of store awnings
hunched at a low lunch
on red kindergarten stools.

With daughters braced between their knees,
masked mothers brake
and lean their scooters
into corners and down the street.

Grooms in black and brides in white,
pose and repose,
before the cathedral
and around the lake and park.

Cobblers sew sandals
on the sidewalk,
and cabbies pull to the curb
as their doors fly open.

Gray-haired men lay
across their motorbike seats,

their shoulders on the handlebars,
taking naps in the morning sun.

Yellow-shirted school children
line-up across the post office steps
displaying promotion cards
as their teacher snaps the moment.

Cruise English

It helps to be young, eager and strong.
Men should be handsome with close cut hair,
and women must welcome pulling theirs back,
even drawn into a tight bun.

Easy smiles are mandatory and secure left hands
to lift loaded trays and move across the deck
between rows of tables and guests' erratic dance.

But most important is easy
Downton Abbey English

> *Good morning, sir.*
> *How are you, madam?*
> *Would you like juice?*
> *Can I remove this?*
> *Would you like anything else?*

Courtesy abounds from rail to rail, stack to keel.
Sunshine and civility spread slick and smooth,
sweet, sumptuous and servile.

Walking through Paradise

Banff Avenue leads to the bridge
across the Bow and to the front gate
of the National Park Service gardens.

Mountains rise left and right,
behind and before, stark faces of bare rock
scraped and smoothed by wind and rain,
snow, ice, and springtime melts.

Here is our vacation jewel,
a place of history and beauty
worth the cost of distant travel –
flights, rental cars, hotels and meals.

We bring hiking boots and cameras
and hope to find snow laden peaks,
blue skies, clouds and pine forest quilts
doubled in the mirroring pane
of undisturbed, sleeping lakes.

But our walk through town
feels like being trapped in a mall
as the holiday season peaks.

At intersections, crowds build like waves,
energy pushing from the back rows,
waiting, waiting, till the light turns
and they can wash over the street,
flood up the facing curb,
and thin across the open sidewalk.

But the open space soon disappears
and we're pressed between the street and store fronts
where shoppers cluster to consider and price
and others stand motionless
in tight islands of nibble and chat,
while, like human eddies, the fast divide,
then curl around and pass the slow.

Postcards don't show these crowds,
and TripAdvisor doesn't rate them.

Golden Silence

In sight of the train tracks
the assurances felt weak,
like a hollow promise
whose surface was glitter thin
and insides echoed.

So we crossed the highway
and drove up a small hill
just above the large lot
where semi-truck-trailers
could park for the night –
an eight-hour limit
of rumbles and groans
but currently empty.

At the top we found a room
away from the road
and far from the elevator.

Sleep is never guaranteed.
It's like ordering a meal
based on the menu's photograph –
something you hope will match
its reputation.

But the chances of dozing off increase
when you drop into a pillow
knowing you're far from the ice machine
and a train won't run through your room.

Fairfield Suites Breakfast

Local thefts, auto sales and storm news
whispers from the flat screen.

A ball-capped team of bricklayers
in scuffed work boots, worn jeans,
and good-morning bright, turquoise t-shirts
chatter in Spanish and laugh
between forkfuls of waffles and sips of coffee.

Three women arrive half awake,
in rumpled pajamas and flapping flip-flops,
their hair still pillow-pinched,
their cheeks sallow and eyes limp
like the Before picture in a Maybelline ad.

An older couple across a narrow table
lean toward each other as he reads
the USA Today's front page
and she nods and moves another link
from her plate to his.

In the soft morning haze outside
small waves of cars and trucks
speed by on their way to the on ramp
or points unknown.

Inside, everyone begins at the corner alcove,
then pauses to survey the counters
laden with coffee and juice, fresh fruit and dry cereal,
oatmeal, fixings, breads, bagels and muffins,
eggs and with grits, bacon and sausage,

and syrup, pancakes, waffles and plates.

Some are moving to the clock,
while others are sipping the spacious nectar
of another vacation pause.

Some eat breakfast, then get on their way.
Others pack their second and third meal.

"Top of the Morning!"

The same smile and kindness.
The same welcome to a shared day
and invitation to make the most
of what we might experience.

But packaged in fresh language,
like traveling through another country
where coffee comes in smaller cups
or evening foods appear for breakfast.

Variety that breaks routine
to reawaken our taste buds and ears,
pay closer attention to the moment –
the taste of a cherry,
a rind of orange,
the good wishes of a stranger.

Turning Tables in Monterey

The economics are simple.
You can have the best chef
and the most inventive menu.

You can win awards,
garner Yelp recommendations,
even install blinking neon
to highlight your location.

But you can't serve more meals
than your tables can hold.

The magic factor, the spice
that feeds the cash drawer,
is how many parties you can sit
at the same table each night.

Everyone needs to feel welcome,
and those who feel rushed
will often refuse to end their story
or hand over a credit card
before they're damned well ready.

So it's a delicate transition
between "Stay as long as you want"
and getting each table cleared and reset.

But at Monterey's Fish House
tables flip faster than a Vegas magician
can pull a quarter from your ear
or turn a dollar into a dove.

When the last guest steps from his chair
and begins his amble toward the door,
the top is wiped clean,
linen, silver, china and crystal are replaced,
and the next party is ushered to their seats
before the previous diners reach the sidewalk.

The wait-staff doesn't announce their next trick,
introduce themselves or receive applause,
but they give a championship performance
as good as the meal
and as inspiring as the California sky.

Tribal Awe

The motels empty as sunset approaches –
some sitting in Adirondack chairs on hillside terraces,
but most crossing Moonstone Drive
and spreading out along the boardwalk,
or following paths down to the beach
to sit on bleached driftwood trunks.

But all are facing west, many with cameras,
some arm in arm, and others leading groups of children,
waiting, waiting for the sun to drop.

The Pacific's white mist blanket
spreads the evening's light like a translucent scrim,
and the sun slowly turns orange
as the horizon nibbles its edge,
first breaking its lower lip,
then munching its way up.

And though we arrive in modern cars,
are beneficiaries of modern medicine,
hoist our cell phones to capture the moment,
and tell friends about our travels,
our communal pause and shared wonder
feels miraculously reassuring
and beautiful to every eye.

Going to O'Hare in Fog

The gauzy white covering the fence
and blurring the roadway as it reaches the curb
is like a skim milk scrim
dampening yesterday's squeals
and bandaging last night's swelter.

On the sidewalk,
away from the electric-eye doors,
a "complimentary-breakfast" cook
takes a long breath as the city awakens,
savoring the clean air that reminds her
of vacations to her Kentucky brother
where mountain ridges greet her at sunrise.

Then our mixed group of limber and lame,
tattooed and unmarked,
polished, trimmed, wild and scuffed
fills every row of the hotel van,
and on our way to Terminal 3
we are members of the same congregation
believing in the myths of technology
and trusting in the good will
of taxi drivers, engineers, and especially pilots
who invite us aboard, then tell us to unplug.

And as our van cuts through the cloudy broth
we sit in meditative silence as if collectively praying
that they know how to study their instruments
when they can't see the runway or fence
and that they will safely take us near the street
where we've parked our dreams.

Passing through First Class

After the parents with children,
those needing extra time,
and active or former military
("Who we thank for their service")
first class flyers are welcomed aboard.

The rest of us line up at stanchions
labelled according to the leg room and width
of the seat we can afford
and how likely we will be
to find open overhead storage
when we arrive at our seat.

It's not a biblical process.
For flights to Atlanta, Newark, Houston and L.A.
the first are first, and the last are last.

And the next several moments feel weird,
as if entering a hotel through a penthouse
where royalty are watching cricket
and sipping afternoon tea.

Most first-classers ignore
the arduous drama of commoners
hauling their backpacks, purses and roller bags,
snacks, sandwiches, neck pillows and presents.

Most preoccupy themselves
reading a crisp newspaper or laptop mail
and sipping a fresh cocktail,
like they might do

shielded behind a limo's smoked glass
on the way to an appointment, lunch or a play.

Their downcast eyes seem self-protective,
like not touching a restroom handle,
as if our presence might infect or erode
their hard-won position.

But there's almost always one
enjoying the luxuries of high place,
yet, perhaps, still connected to us all.

She looks up, eye to eye,
nods or smiles a quiet welcome,
and it is comforting to know
that beyond the mesh, stay-out curtain
in the corridors of power, linen napkins,
fresh fruit and wine,
there may be a big-hearted ally
who will help us all board the raft
if we suffer a water landing.

Homecoming

At last, the runway roar lifted us
like an express elevator racing to arrive
for a late reservation in a tower restaurant

where we were fed an appetizer plate
of pearl lights and neon ribbons
over a quiet bed of crushed velvet

and the evening's special was a medley
of freshly broiled, locally sourced heat lightning
auditioning around swings of the kitchen door.

And after a long day of landing, laundry, and mail,
thanks to the Main Street Merchants Association,
we shucked and planted our chairs in the parking lot

among the burgeoning rows of excess workers,
a stuffed supply yard of tired talent
eager for another helping of rock, blues, twist and
    Motown,

and like an inter-denominational homecoming,
where slick tuxes and crinoline gowns were forbidden
and t-shirts, Bermudas, grey hair and bald spots were par,

we caught the waves and broad smiles of friends we'd
    missed,
weaved our way through the agility course of legs, canes,
    coolers and dancers,
and felt reborn in each sweaty embrace, damp kiss, and
    "Welcome back!"

Eight Minutes
& Forty-Six Seconds

Painting

We used to stand and sing together
at the ballpark, in the seventh inning stretch.

"America, America" climbed and grew
while the words reminded us
of the vast plains, peaks, and flowing rivers

that lay like an artist's palette
in the collective hands of the people –

a big-hearted, generous crowd,
working together, painting the dream
that hung in our shared living room.

We used to stand and sing.
We used to feel together.

Table Talk
for A.C.

At lunch we touch on love,
love of country and the flag —
standing for the anthem,
removing your hat and singing along,
even putting your hand over your heart.

"If they don't respect the flag, they can leave."

"But, but, but..."
The list goes on and on.

> What about the freedom of speech
> and the right to peaceful protest?

> What about wanting a better country —
> a place where people of color
> aren't disproportionately victimized
> and sometimes killed by police?

> Can't one be loyal, appreciative
> and still desire more and better?

> And even if you're a blessed star athlete,
> shouldn't you enjoy the same right
> to take a stand in public view?

I wipe the quesadilla grease from my fingers
and reach across the salad,
hoping a handshake will bridge the rift
and keep our friendship whole.

Others appear uncomfortable,
like we're on a raft about to flip.

They encourage silence
then steer the conversation
back to safer ground:

the way doctors are often wrong,
whether the golf course will haul off windfalls,
and if Disney can continue to expand.

Universal Inattention

So a few true believers
go on a Parisian shooting spree,
proving that Mohammed's image is lethal,
and thousands gather with pens in the air,
declaring, "*Je suis Charlie.*"

They march. They shout.
They try to rally our concern.

But we need to protect our freedoms
and gather by the thousands
to indulge our Universal Studios right
to over-amplified music,
excess fat, personal scooters,
and constant distraction
from the world beyond our shores.

To What?

I pledge allegiance
to the principles of freedom from tyranny
with respect and opportunity for all.

It's not the flag.
That's just a symbol of an idea —
that a country can be formed
based on codes of fairness and love,
openness and welcome.

And that "under God" bit
just doesn't fit
because it can be another form of intolerance
and self-righteous manipulation.

Let's keep it clean.
Let's keep it simple.

Take a knee, raise a fist,
or even stand tall, remove your hat,
and place your hand over your heart.

But let's unite for a just cause,
not for some dogmatic perversion
or racist masquerade.

Eight Minutes and Forty-Six Seconds
In memory of George Floyd (1973-2020)

Eight minutes and forty-six seconds
is enough time to unload a dishwasher,
walk around the block,
say your vows, kiss your bride
and walk up the aisle.

It's sufficient
for deciding what's right and wrong,
asking for a breath,
speaking to your mother,
and changing your mind.

In this span one can light a fire,
acknowledge systemic racism,
recite the names of victims,
and decide that enough is enough.

During the ticking we can remember
that America is a fragile idea,
peaceful protest is a right,
police are not above the law,
and empathy knits communities together
while only bullies seek to dominate.

There's room in eight minutes and forty-six seconds
to tell a complex story,
decide that the future must be better,
and start to make that happen.

Passing Through

Clean Pants

Freshly washed jeans hug my legs
and girdle my waist.
The button hole and stud

behave like feuding neighbors
and need a tug across my belly's street
before they're forced to shake hands.

And each pocket is similarly unaccommodating.
My handkerchief has a reservation in the left rear,
but the door is tightly closed

and I need to force it in to get it seated.
On mornings like this
I check the mirror or step on the scale

to see if I'm getting fat.
But I'm just myself garbed in American Casual,
the un-pleated bridge between rich and poor.

And as the hours pass the weave relaxes,
as if attending fabric yoga
where space is breathed into each pocket
and comfort is restored.

Modern Art

Watching twenty-somethings
push their carts to their cars
it's clear there are no more secrets –
no need to wonder or imagine.

Fashion has fully embraced
skin-tight fabrics that cling
to each crotch and crevice,
each belly, bum, nipple and swell.

No more modesty requiring a special key,
like a soft leaning in and whispered *Yes*
before undoing each protective button
and drawing a blouse back for a better view.

Now everyone's invited to the parking lot gallery,
and nothing's hidden beneath the designer's paint.
Just pure art moving with every step and turn,
each reach and lift and bow.

Between Sets

The band takes a break.
Customers cluster outside the door
waiting for the night to cool.

A fuzzy half-moon beams behind a gauzy sky,
but parking lot lights hide the stars
while crickets sing a shrill serenade.

Only a few parking spaces are empty,
and most plates are local.

I walk the lot
hoping to quiet the ringing in my ears.

The weekend has begun.

Lowcountry Off-Roading

Once rice fields. Now waterfowl refuges.
Layovers for migrating flocks.

Dawn to 9:00 breakfast included.
No need for reservations.
Check-out as you wish.

We drive US 17 South
along the Carolina Birding Trail
and pull off at brown signs
leading to rutted dirt roads
over long-abandoned dikes.

From wildlife watchtowers
looking over the sheets of still water
and scatterings of resident ducks,
we hear the continuous hum of tires
spinning across the near interstate cement.

I ask the hostess at Skipper's Fish Camp,
"What's there to do in Darien?"

She replies in unedited certainty,
"Nothing! Just sit and enjoy the sun."

Sunday Quiet

Some days there's too much wind
or lawn crews blowing leaves
to enjoy the white screen silence.

But when the lagoon wears a mirror face
in the noon of a work-free Sunday
the quiet extends its welcome
far beyond what's seen.

The gunwale knock of paddles
comes long before the canoes appear.

The whisper of tires crossing the bridge
threads its way through the trees.

Birds call from distant branches.
Motors whirr and pause.

Then disembodied conversations
about the distance to the green
precede each cart.

MOTOvation

*for Wedgefield's **M**en **O**n **T**heir **O**wn*

Each waitress smiles when we say, "One check,"
then circles the table taking drink orders
as we scan the menu and discuss daily specials.

It's a ritual as casual as combing hair
or walking down the drive near dawn
to retrieve the morning paper.

We're not there for serious work,
and the meal's just another kind of clock,
something advancing in stages
till we pay the bill and know it's time to leave.

From the first handshake to the last goodbye
we're practicing the art of chumminess –
being easy friends sharing stories
and bits of current news
like paging through a weekly paper –
headlines on hurricanes or home repair,
box scores of favorite teams or stocks,
and a glance at recent comics,
but always treading cautiously near editorials
to keep the group intact.

The cost of real estate creates some commonality.
Everyone can travel and leave a hefty tip.
But like every classroom of every school,
homogeneity is a myth, and difference is everywhere.

So we still need to reach to imagine

growing in another place, working another job
and what it might feel like
to have different children, wives and skills.

But when we part,
the week feels more complete,
the street in better repair,
and the world a bit more in tune.

Farmed Out

Main Street has lost its luster.
Auto repair holds hands with tire shops,
fast teriyaki is dating authentic Mexican flavor,
and Tony's Ice Cream is sandwiched
between music and pawn shops -
all of them bedded in crumbling asphalt
near sprouts of lonely chicory and uneven sandstone slabs.

The Methodist steeple lifts its pure white needle
above the distant rise, and behind double-walled Plexiglas
and the pass-through drawer for IDs, checks,
cash and deposit slips,
the Bank of America teller offers broad-smiled help.

Money has walked from the city center
and left indoor malls to gray-haired walkers,
Halloween masks, sports apparel, and discount shoes.

In former pastures near interstate exits,
new investors have planted outlet malls
with undulating walls of mauve, cream and gray
complementing the fieldstone planters
and brick and sculptured concrete walks
surrounding a central fountain
where three-year-olds run and face-off
as their mothers rest from stroller pushing.

Here everyone mingles and says, "Excuse me,"
as they seek a steal, the latest fashion,
or another favorite for their already full closet.

And a small army of landscape workers,
clip, prune and weed the manicured gardens
surrounding the alphabetized parking lot
with signs showing the route back to the highway.

"Road Fish" Closed

Big projects, with wrecking balls and bulldozers,
follow the formalities.

"The Something Corporation is pleased to announce
the wedding of fresh capital and another developer's
    dream.
Services to be held early next fall."

Then the press feasts at hearings,
neighbors write letters to the editor,
headlines scream and photographers click.

And the cranes only arrive long after
the flagging and fencing are in place.

But small changes come with a shock.

Around each bend, normal soothes the eye.
Then it's tossed into unwanted reverie
when fresh craft paper drapes each window
and murky shadows show where the sign used to be.

"Gone?" we ask.
"Gone!" we wonder.

Caught in the grip of that surprise,
I recall walking the showroom,
reviewing the baskets and clips,
handgrips, lights and mirrors
left behind for another day,
and the counter and bike stand

where it was so easy to adjust my brakes.

The memory echoes
in an emptied corner of my heart.

Like so many other minnows,
this one swam away.

My Vertical Neighborhood

A square brown post
ascends above the dock bench
waiting for a bluebird.
Shit and beauty always arrive.

≈ ≈ ≈

Palm trunks line the fairway.
Green moss speckles each north side.
Fronds above dance with the wind
and remain in balance during every shot.

≈ ≈ ≈

Players stand above the ball,
still, silent, set - frozen in thought,
then flail and nearly fall
as their dreams again depart.

≈ ≈ ≈

Dark pilings rise above the water.
Their cousins shimmer below.
They support the bridge from bank to bank.
I call my siblings every second month.

≈ ≈ ≈

Branching crepe myrtle hides the bay.
Only bits of cars and kayaks
show through its feathery arms.
Neighborliness trumps weed control.

≈ ≈ ≈

Each blade lifts and dips in rocking rhythm
as the kayaks move forward
to a hull-thumping beat.
Small steps in a long journey.

Passing Through

I arrive at the shore without attachments,
no favorite seat or place
clinging to some distant memory.
Every spot offers a fresh view.

This morning's breeze brings its sole identity,
and any chair is as good as another
if unoccupied, in enough sun to take off the chill,
and not so dirty my pants will be spoiled.

Across the water a pier stretches
into the sound at an obtuse angle
above a crosshatch of pilings
shedding fresh reflections.

Many stroll the seawalk nearby –
young couples brushing shoulders,
a man with a beer gut, tight T-shirt and beret,
two ladies stepping slowly in Sunday finery,
one with a cane, the other with a lavender scarf.

Each is a new invention on familiar themes,
but their true histories remain hidden,
and I can only guess as confident and insecure
as squirting oil toward a hidden hinge.

And like life's other rarely visited terminals –
the airports, bus stops, open houses, and happy hours –
I'm only passing through and can leave it be.

There's no need to sweep or heal,
no demand to comfort, build, deepen or maintain.

Just freedom to breathe
and pause a moment in this gallery,
noting the art on display, the music being played,
and the uncertain stories spawned
by each sweater, flip-flop, belt and smile.

House Hunting

Each door swings smoothly,
and we enter clean hallways and spotless rooms,
with lights turned on,
and sometimes soft background music.

Every surface has been wiped and polished.
All lingering clutter is hidden,
stuffed in closets, cupboards or drawers,
so our eyes and imagination
can roam and feast on the open space,
the light entering the clear windows,
the view of pines across the fairway,
and the sparkle off granite counter tops.

We explore with our shopping list in mind —
room for overnight guests,
an area for quiet conversations,
places for desks, a retreat, a pool table,
and more, and more, and more.

Like traversing a forest holding a rifle or camera,
every hunt brings surprises —
an organized filing system tucked in a closet,
several approaches to storing shoes,
a palatial desk facing a huge flat screen,
bikes hanging from the garage ceiling,
water gurgling over a rock shelf
in a small bowl on the wet bar.

Like taking clothes off the rack,
finding an open dressing room,

and looking in the mirror to see what fits,
if the cut's too loose or tight, too short or long,
we keep a watchful eye on our inner selves
and on each other's face and voice
when reassembling around the kitchen island.

Is this the spot for our next adventure?
What might we learn just being here?
Do we want to leave or stay?

Break Point!

In Memory of Peter Rosenberg
March 18, 1945 – November 18, 1988

He bounced into our life,
halfback happy, cat-gut tough.

He moved like pro's--
jetting 'cross continents,
out-slicing opponents,
befriending fans.

We had such a sporting time,
sprinting through Sunday papers,
benching Nixon,
leaning sweat into each other
as the basketball pop-corned about the rim,
mapping bombs that snow-numbed fingers
                    might yet snag,
                    might sting and drop,
lounging around the chess board.

And now,
          break point,
he's got
          a handball tumor.

In the Underworld

I hope the squirrels are happy.
I feel attacked.

Autumn arrived with vengeance.
Leaves clogged gutters and drains.
Yards oozed, and puddles spread.
Then the oaks began their assault.

Acorns, acorns everywhere –
smacking the pavement,
battering the windshield,
and denting our car's roof.

I relish their crunch beneath my boot
but take each concussion-threatened stroll
cautiously seeking open spaces
to enjoy the chill and changing color.

Hose

Mine is an un-fanged
North American Yellow Stripe
with a trigger head that will spit in your eye
if you drop it by a pail.

It climbs fenders, curls around tires,
and only coils to the right.

Not Yet

Crows cluster and forage in the fairway,
paying no attention to the rushing clouds
or muscle-shirted southern wind.

Air drags across my face and forearms
like a soaked washcloth leaving a moist film,
underscoring the thunderstorm watches

that scrolled below The Memorial's final holes,
and I'm still waiting for the first drops
to christen yesterday's freshly nailed decking.

I had hoped to start my day
with coffee, headlines, and a paint brush
drawing a grey coat over the raw, yellow boards.

But each hour has passed at an uneventful creep,
and though the sky darkened before happy hour
and early bird orders have already been served,

fishermen are still in their canoes,
sculling their bows into the breeze,
baiting hooks and casting into the reeds,

while a great blue heron with ruffled feathers
stands on a dock railing like an ashen sentry,
as inert as a statue of calm and patience.

A deep rumble seems to report the approaching storm
but builds into a roar trailing the silhouetted specks
of two fighter jets between the clouds.
And the waiting stretches on and on.

Holiday Herds

Reindeer have descended with the dark.

They stand on shelves,
cluster on the dining room table,
pose in white silhouettes
before green flood lights,
and leap through pine forests
on napkins and towels.

One loaned his antlers to our mailbox.
Another gave his to a red VW Beetle
driven by a bright-eyed woman
with short white hair
and a broad, broad smile.

Our lawns have gone to sleep.
The trees have shed their leaves.

But the deer hang around
in darkness, dawn and midday,
unafraid of dogs or hunters,
never asking for food or drink,
just reminding us of days on the farm
where we never lived
and delivery myths before FedEx.

Robin in Fog

Starbucked

Caffeine connects us
on high tops and squares,
with laptops flipped open,

in untucked, unbuttoned,
un-ironed shirts and shorts

or sport coats, shiny shoes
and bright silk handkerchiefs
trying to escape breast pockets.

Some nibble dry berry scones.
Others lick their sticky fingers.

But all have an obligatory cup,
warmed, stirred and waiting
within easy reach.

The lovers and lonely,
friends, family and conspirators,
partners, sharks and targets,

bunched together
like attending morning mass,
rubbing sleep from our eyes,
squinting into the light of a new day.

Unfinished Shopping

I know it's not part of their normal training
or as easy as pointing to an aisle,
but I'd leave the store more complete
if cashiers could solve my mysteries
while swiping barcodes and taking my cash.

Instead, I often push my cart under the electric eye
and load bags in the trunk
still trying to link a smile to a home,
a face to a place.

The supermarket doesn't offer enough clues.
People arrive in other clothes
or with spouses I've never seen,
and there's no logic connecting
a pause at olives or squeezing bananas
to where someone works or what they do.

So late into the following night,
long after the parking lot's cleared,
carts have been snaked and guided indoors,
and I've placed every purchase
in its proper drawer, shelf or bowl,
that unidentified face still festers
in my memory's cupboard.

those deep brown eyes

they speak to me
they call from shadows
ceaselessly

I bend an ear
to hear their call
to see their gleam
to yet recall

your scent, your touch
your loving grace
the longing look
upon your face

and tenderly
you still are there
op'ning your arms
and bidding fair

that I embrace
and hold you tight
all through the day
all through the night

and eager I
jump in the dream
ever hoping
that it will seem

reality
for me, for you
for all, for ever
for now, for *nous*

Sweater Scented

Distracted by music
and thoughts of the day ahead,
slipping hands down snug sleeves
and tugging the knitted snowstorm
over my tunneling head,
sweater scented you returned,
sweetly entering my body,
sucked and savored belly deep.

Sweetness on sweetness,
again and again.

Your touch lingering on my shoulder.
Your smile eye to eye.
Your laughter in the distance.

Shadowy images in the bathroom glare.
Fireside warmth over the chill morning tile.

Together
for Barbara

I was lost and you offered directions.
I felt cold and you shared a blanket.

I was hungry and we ate.
I felt lonely and we walked and talked.

I was tired and we slept.
When bored, we told stories,
played games, sang and danced.

We wept and laughed
and laughed and laughed.

I was grateful
when you accepted my kiss.

Robin in Fog

Even birds feel alone and wait
as the grey softens calls
and hides the next tree.

Even birds sit still and silent
in the damp chill,
knowing, perhaps praying,
the sun will slowly restore the day.

Even birds.

With William in the House
for William Demir Özdemir

We eat, talk and travel
in the niches between his needs.

Like the sun and the moon,
our day's tide ebbs and flows
between the push and pull
of his hunger and fatigue.

And in it all we wonder
how much is getting through.

We babble and coo,
sing, dance and chatter,
tell stories and show,
touch, poke and after
we hope for a smile,
a glance or a stare
and then we must
leave it there.

We know these days
will soon be forgotten.
He will roll and crawl,
name, walk, talk and run,
take, make, break and build,
read, explore and more.

And across the years, he will stare
from the corner of photographs,
again and again and again,
where we hope he will stand tall,
have his arm around friends and family,
look out at the world with confidence and joy,
and someday – maybe, someday –
do it again for his own.

Closed

My pen likes to wander
by classrooms and stores,
up church aisles and garden paths,
through bedrooms and meals,
into caves and storms and moonless nights.

It's taken me down many dark alleys,
into hidden corners of adolescence,
indecision, disgust and doubt.

And sometimes I've escaped with humor
or found a freshly powered flashlight
that helped me climb stairwells to new understanding.

But some doors remain firmly closed,
and even if I can peek through the keyhole
I'm hesitant to pick the lock,
raise the shades and schedule an open house.

Some stories are beyond the razor-wire
and should stay there.

Super Moon

It was a heavy felt gray sky
with only a few stars,
and having finished dinner
they were headed to their car.

"You came for the super moon,"
she said, "too bad!
Yesterday was spectacular,
but there's nothing now."

So we embraced,
shared news,
and made plans
for later that week.

And we walked down the beach steps
and crossed the loose sand
to the water's edge,
where high tide was clamoring
and throwing sea grass at our feet.

Then, in the distant dimness,
a slice of orange
slowly peeled into view,
and we stood quietly side by side,
relishing the tangy smell,
sipping its sweetness,
and pouring drops of its pebbled juice
into our camera.

How to Hold a Pencil

First, keep it close,
like in your car's console,
in your pocket or on a nightstand,
where you can reach it
without having to search or wait.

Pick it up with gratitude
for the word or phrase you have in mind
and curiosity about what will come.

Your body should be relaxed,
your posture comfortable
where you can take full breaths
and let them out, smooth as cream.

Place your fingers on its shaft
as if measuring its pulse –
the way a fisherman holds a rod
to feel the tug of what is hidden
and guess if he's in an abundant place
or needs to cast elsewhere.

Let each word flow from its tip,
letter by letter, syllable by syllable,
as you record your inner voice
offering the next and next possibility.

And as the phrases arrive
use your pencil like an oar
guiding it in and around snags and dead falls,
through shoots between boulders

over the bubbles of rushes
and into and across pools of calm.

When you think you may be done, pause and wait,
sliding your fingers along its smooth, clean length,
like gauging the weight of a favorite jewel,
and seeing what sparkles are left
before you decide to set it down
and turn the spigot off.

"But It's Not Like That Anymore"

Some say it was the front porch.
The need to escape the heat
before air conditioning brought us back indoors.
And sitting outside meant meeting and greeting,
seeing each other, learning names and faces,
knowing children and sharing concerns.

Every street had a hundred eyes,
and parents shared the burden
of sweeping kids back home
and guiding them toward good.

At least that's the picture on history's mantle.
That's the day we miss –
a black-and-white community of shared purpose and trust.

The criminals and pedophiles didn't show up for the shot.
They hid in backrooms and basements,
plotting who to rob and rape.

But it's not like that anymore.

Now we distrust everyone,
watch our news alone,
stay inside, lock our doors,
and teach our kids to beware.

No more street ball
or kick-the-can before dark,
running through back yards,
climbing over fences and hiding in bushes.

We don't want to annoy our neighbors,
and they sure better not mess with our kids.

Us

A wave, a shout across the fairway.
A window-down pause in the road,
to say, "Hello. Safe travels. Have fun."

A glance, a hug, a wink –
the tiny steps to us.

Meet for coffee. Share a beer.
Pop a cork. Walk the beach.
Start a book club. Rub shoulders, doubts.
Share stories of loss across the years.

University Still Life

University Still Life

The welcome gate is closed,
guard's kiosk empty.

Though reserved 7:00-5:00,
faculty spaces lay fallow.
Not a single car claims a spot
or waits for its owner's return.

One leaf tumbles
across the open asphalt
toward the distant curb.

The Student Union's silent –
tables and chairs stacked,
silverware trays empty,
serving platters washed and waiting.
Dust gathers on the open floor.

A blue jay flits
from branch to soil
at a statue's base.

The frame of a soccer goal
waits for a net, a team and ball.
Sun and wind play in the field.

Walkways lead from dorms to classrooms,
but no one rises, sits at desks or labors in labs.

The library remains studiously quiet,
every screen blank and page unturned.

The stadium's jaws open wide –
each seat free, scoreboard blank, band missing.

Summer Entertaining

When they arrive, we stand back
and offer to mask ourselves
if they'd prefer.

We want them to feel comfortable
and create space for them to pass
without a hug or kiss.

We're lucky.

Our back deck is large, our table wide,
and there's no chance of rain,
so we can stay outside, sit far apart,
and let the conversation amble.

We might offer a glass of wine,
a beer or flavored water,
but no cheese or crackers,
no fruit, no nuts, no dip.

Winter will be tough, our living room empty,
without a vaccine to bring us close.

Snow will mound on the drive and deck
while our summer garden takes a rest.

Pandemic Precaution

No more hugs, handshakes or kisses.
Even those that feel
apathetically routine,

like boxed crackers as an appetizer
instead of something artful that took hours
to prepare and arrange just so.

Now doors are closing.
Parties are shutting down,
and soon the bowling alley will go silent.

No more cradle, carry, swing and release
ending in a distant smash and clatter.
No more standing over the shoulder

of a teammate or score keeper
and moving in close
to whisper advice.

Twenty seconds scrubbing knuckles,
drawing suds through finger gaps,
and back and forth across each back and heel
feels like forever.

And elbow bumps are as unfulfilling
as dry bread sandwiches
without the meat.

Azaleas are in bloom. Trees are starting to bud.
Birds are singing, and daylight's inching

farther and farther into night.

But we're headed indoors,
as if fleeing sleet.

There better be another dawn
after this dark night.

Senior Hours at Zagara's

We get up early since the time is short,
then masked and gloved
stand outside before 7:30,
waiting for the doors
to be unlocked.

Shopping carts are lined up inside,
already cleaned and disinfected,
but a supply of alcohol wipes
waits for those needing
to do it themselves.

Only a few workers are there,
unboxing produce, restocking meats,
shelving fresh breads and cakes,
and like a pinball kicking
from bumper to bell, buzzer to flipper,
we dart to our standard staples –
from blueberries to cereal,
OJ to creamer, tortillas and spaghetti.

We pass through most aisles alone
but occasionally break or reverse ourselves
when another couple enters the far end
or huddles together debating some purchase.

We miss the children taking rides
and the teens in flip flops
stopping for sandwiches and sodas.

And instead of a let-me-help-you

and have-you-ever-tried-this stroll
we move at a get-in-and-get-out sprint,
touching as few surfaces as possible
and keeping our distance
from the cashier and bagger
the other side of the acrylic shields.

Yesterday's Oars

Security Questions

My file drawers weren't working.
Rollers were jammed, and I couldn't find my key.

I had placed my trust in safe choices –
my maternal grandfather's first name,
the street where we lived when I was born,
the school where I finished first grade.

Then, on a recorded call
"to improve customer service,"
after my name, social security number and address,
I couldn't remember an answer.

It's worse than moving,
leaving an old neighborhood,
having to find new friends, stores and restaurants.

Discovering the new is easy.
But the old slips out of memory
without a word of goodbye.

And when we try to summon it,
we're shocked by how bare
our room has become.

Parked

I'm sitting at a silent desk
waiting for the opening hour.

My files are packed in a clean case,
prints dusted, memory wiped,
and I'm waiting to ship them
to my new computer.

But the correct cable
is missing.

Crows outside caw from the roof tops
and swoop to the driveway
for a quick drink.

Their lives go on simply –
one coat, no luggage.
Look for food, eat, flock.
Stay out of the rain.

We build tools for all occasions,
then lose a key or password
and get stuck in a parking lot
searching for the missing part.

Lampke's Stained Glasses

He said that there are patterns everywhere –
in books, museums, shops and cathedrals.
So there's no need for originality,
just a lifetime's collection
of tools, glass, copper foil, flux and solder.

Yes, you do need a plan,
some design placed on two templates,
one intact and the other in pieces,
like your vision of a satisfying life
and the fragments of dinners and conversations,
jobs, friendships, travels and pastimes
that might eventually complete the puzzle.

But success demands surrender,
giving in to accidents,
to the reality of never being in full control,
for as carefully as you score and then tap a pane,
like life it can fracture in unexpected places
that demand a fresh approach to beauty.

In the end, everything is built with patience,
leftover pieces, and nicks and cuts along the way,
and though labelled "stained,"
it's not about flaws blemishing purity.

The goal is to find an inspiring light
and let it shine through.

Yesterday's Oars

I used to love the soothing, slippery feeling
of reaching into a sink of warm, soapy water
and searching for the next plate
beneath the bubble cloud.

I'd carefully pinch the rim and slide its face
halfway through the surface
and swirl the sponge around its front and back
before passing it under the faucet's stream
and standing it next to its sisters
stacked in the drying rack.

Then, in the name of efficiency,
we bought a dishwasher,
and I was liberated
from this age-old chore
that connected me
to my youth, my parents and those before.

A fire no longer burns deep into the night,
and few of us can remember a tune
or tell a many-chaptered story
to bring the dark alive.

We've been set free and adrift
in an electronic ocean without yesterday's oars
and only the vaguest notion
of how to read the stars.

Seasonal Overture

The edge of rain arrives
like a flood of minnows
nibbling water bugs bank to bank.

It enters silently,
then begins a pianissimo patter,
a soft and gentle Wagnerian backdrop

for a crow's distant caw
and the dark silhouette of a lone seagull,
a black puppet flapping across a bright sky

ahead of the wispy tendrils of grey
spreading their thin fingers
over the retreating golf carts.

On Seeing Donald Hall's Photograph

His gnarly hands, like mine will be,
rest crossed on the head of a dark maple cane.

His hair flairs, like a wild, misshapen halo
that hasn't been near the aura shop,
a dab of conditioner,
or a comb for years.

His eyes, like small jewels dropped
into the creviced plate of his face,
glow like sunlight
passing through a goblet of cabernet.

Time has drawn its interest
and left a meagre principal.

But the poems stay young,
the pain raw,
the joy juicy and filling.

Haiku Workshop

"Maybe take out the *and,*
or delete the adjective."

"But I like *rosy*.
Without it the sky's colorless."

Tinker, tinker – suggestions swirled.
The tiny poems grew and shrank.
Lines got chopped, married or moved.
Some were added. Some were struck.

But between the lines
sleeping stories raised their heads
and rolled out of bed.

Diagnoses and deaths.
Treasured moments and dementia.
Care-taking and hospitalizations.
Birthdays missed and comic books destroyed.

The stuff of life that follows us
to each new home,
and travels with our luggage
on every vacation.

Tales that needed adjectives and articles,
personal pronouns and space to breathe.

Stories that couldn't wear petite
and begged for more than seventeen.

First Ladies at Ruby Lee's

The first ladies on the dance floor
stay there all night.

Their skin glistens red near the Exit sign,
and their eyes lock on the lead singer
as if taking vows.

"You are mine, and I am yours.
Take me now. Take me please."

The floor crowds with dancers,
but they hold their turf.

One hip-sways and leans
into a shoulder shimmy,
then back in a syncopated pause.

The other bounces
in search of each rhythm
that her feet never find.

The decades pass in familiar choruses,
as we rock in our seats
and lip-read comments.

Swirls of energy devour our waitress,
and Sports Center replays populate the screens.

Hands shoot to Love Shack thumps,
as dancers twirl, jump and swim.

But when others drop, wet and exhausted,
the first ladies refuse to sit.

"He's got to see what's in this dress,
and I've got plenty of time."

Photography 201: Selfies

Smartphones in every hand,
on every bridge and stair,
in each park and chapel,
at every meal and market.

Here's a beautiful picture.
  Now, add me.

Here's a miraculous fresco.
  Now, add me.

I took a trip and saw the canyon.
  Look. I'm there.

No more waste or mess,
carving initials into a tree or desk,
spray painting a bare wall.

Look at that tower,
the canal and statue.
  See, I was wearing blue,
  and the wind whipped my hair.

I know, this one is truly amazing.
Took them three centuries to complete.
  And don't you think
  that's a good picture of me?

  Yes, I do too.

Getting the Paper before Sunrise

When the days of wind and rain departed,
they left behind a clean sky
where, like a lonely headlight,

a high-beam moon cast crisp,
murder mystery shadows
across the driveway,

and only a few of the strongest stars
kept their lights on.

And in the deep surrounding stillness
there wasn't a chirp or rustle,
just the moan of distant motors
reaching across the miles.

Reading Lucille Clifton

Only a few people know how
to celebrate each small part –

toenails and eyelashes,
an extra ten minutes of sleep,
the pad of butter on a hot potato,
a friend's quiet generosity,

the clenched fist forever raised
above the Olympics' award ceremony.

No hardship keeps her silent.
Her song has room for it all.

A Sonneteer's Complaint

I need to find a pentameter line
that I can use to kick this into moving.
I rarely write in such a metered time
and find the task both rough and so eluding.

I've read and voiced two tons of Shakespeare's work.
You'd think I'd have the cadence mastered now
and could draft as fast as coffee perks.
But no! My brain this magic won't allow.

It balks. It halts. It stumbles word to word
in jerky thoughts and awkward jumps from phrase
to phrase, with rhythm just, but ideas slurred,
and far from work deserving any praise.

The day has passed. This poem is close to done,
and soon I'll leave for cocktail hour and fun.

Plan It Backwards

The side of the green for the easiest putt,
the favorite pitch shot,
the driver or fairway wood, hybrid or iron
that will deliver the ball to that spot.

Yard waste up front – close to the driver's seat,
cardboard under bagged garbage,
and recyclables behind, close to the back door
where I'll stand after parking
just past the dump's entrance.

The freshest lettuce below,
newest creamer in back.

The hardest question in reserve,
behind dinner and small talk,
an appetizer and first drink.

What could be a last illness
after revising a will, updating a trust,
taking a walk about town
and writing this poem.

Photos

Front Cover – Descending Walkway, Gubbio, Perugia, Italy**

p. 1 – Turbid Sky, Palmetto Dunes Lagoon, Hilton Head Island, South Carolina*

p. 27 – Ancient Frieze, Angkor Thom, Cambodia**

p. 55 – Alhambra Fortress Gun Port, Granada, Spain*

p. 63 – Giant Cedars Hiking Trail, Mount Revelstoke National Park, British Columbia, Canada**

p. 86 – Robin in Fog, Hilton Head Island, South Carolina*

p. 96 – William Demir Özdemir*

p. 103 – Vacant Campus, John Carroll University, University Heights, Ohio*

p. 113 – Paddle Rack, Ojibway Family Lodge (Keewaydin Camp), Lake Temagami, Ontario, Canada*

Back Cover – Maligne Canyon, Jasper National Park, Alberta, Canada.*

Photos by Barbara Hill-Newby (**) and Bill Newby (*).

Appreciations

In an early draft of an editors' note for an anthology, Sansing McPherson wrote that "Writers are solitary creatures." Yes, we sit alone and need to be free of distractions to find the right words for the next line, sentence, stanza or paragraph. But our work is also fostered by those with whom we share and collaborate.

This is true of the poems in this collection, leaving me indebted to many who have graciously read or listened to drafts and offered reactions and encouragement. Among these are the following:

In addition to the many fellow poets with whom I've workshopped, I'm grateful for the poetic insights of my workshop leaders: Stephen Dunn and Tony Hoagland (Chautauqua Writers Festival), Dorianne Laux and Aimee Nezhukumatathil (Palm Beach Poetry Festival), and Ray McNiece (Lit Cleveland).

On Hilton Head Island, I was fortunate to be welcomed into the Island Writers' Network's community where I benefitted from monthly speakers, workshops, and open mics, and had the opportunity to explore editing and producing three anthologies. Thank you to all IWN members for your stimulation and insight, and especially to Elizabeth Abrams, Sallie Collins, Art Cornell, Barry Dickson, Marijanet Doonan, Suzie Eisinger, Eric Johnson, Miho Kinnas, Norm Levy, Phil Lindsey, James Mallory, John McIlroy, Sansing McPherson, Kerry Peresta and Elizabeth Robin.

In addition, I want to thank all of the poets who joined the annual Kick-Start Poetry Readings and to my dear friend, Audre Allison, who hosted many series of writing workshops through Lifelong Learning of Hilton Head Island and who joined me for many lunches where we shared poetry and stories.

Returning to Cleveland during a pandemic made networking with other writers challenging. Therefore, I am grateful to Cuyahoga County Public Library for hosting poetry workshops and readings and to Lit Cleveland's array of literary workshops and events. My Cleveland return was especially enhanced by my new "2nd Wednesday" poetry friends whose work continues to grow.

Furthermore, in Cleveland I am very lucky to be closer to Adrian Schnall, my colleague in letters, who I can always rely on for an honest, thorough, and inventive reading of any wobbling poem.

Last and most importantly, I owe untold thanks to Barbara Hill-Newby, my first reader, toughest critic, and companion, who has consistently supported and improved my life and writing.

About the Author

Bill Newby was born and raised in Cleveland, Ohio where he worked as an English teacher, high school administrator, college advisor and adjunct lecturer. After six years in South Carolina, he and his wife, Barbara Hill-Newby, returned to Cleveland.

He considers himself an "everyday writer" using poetry and fiction to record and explore moments of celebration, complaint, concern and comedy.

His work has appeared in *Blue Mountain Review, Bluffton Breeze*; Gordon Square Review: *Neighborhood Voices*; Island Writers' Network's *Time & Tide, Ebb & Flow*, and *Reflections* anthologies; *Ohio Teachers Write*; the *Palm Beach Poetry Festival Fish Tales Contest*; *Panoplyzine*; *Sixfold*; *Spine Line*; and *Whiskey Island*.

Sea Chests or a Carry-On (2018), a first collection, is available from Amazon and can be previewed at www.billnewby.net.

Bill can be reached at: Bill.Newby.wordsmith@gmail.com

Praise for *Sea Chests or a Carry-On*

Bill Newby writes poems about friendship, nature, family, and everyday life with a rhythmic cadence that makes you see life through a new lens. He has a unique style, and he celebrates the quiet moments one might easily overlook. I love the imagery he brings to life as he weaves a story. [He] is a masterful writer, a keen observer of life, and a beautiful photographer. You can read these poems over and over, and you will see something different each time. Enjoy!
– *Hilary S. Williams*

Bill Newby's poetry captures and transforms small everyday sights and occurrences turning the ordinary into exciting bits of life we often miss. I linger and smile at the treat. He also deals profoundly with major events, always finding new ways of looking and thinking. It is life being lived, taking stock of the value or the fun of everything when awareness awakens. I also love the way he is using a lot of self-invented form and random rhyme so beautifully, swelling rhythm and sound.
– *Audre Allison*

My husband and I spent a most enjoyable evening reading Bill's poems to each other. *Sea Chests or a Carry-On* is a gem of a book – heartfelt and filled with universal themes. You will want to have this book in your personal library. It is also the perfect gift for those special people in your life.
– *Barbara Bellassai*

Bill Newby is an astute observer of everyday life. He is able to take ordinary events and life experiences and translate them into thoughtful and entertaining poems.
– *Robert Weast*

Bill Newby takes notice and informs the reader about everyday life from both a wide angle and very close up. Each poem is a real treat.
– *Denny Baer*

Sea Chests or a Carry-On is a stunning collection. I was surprised by how tidy, concise, and detailed the poems are. I loved how well they created and evoked an entire moment with just a few words or a single line. They were humorous, serious, contemplative, and evoked memories of a full and interesting life. One of my favorite things about poetry is when specific details of a memory or a moment in time are shared it feels like a personal invitation and connection. So many of these poems accomplished that for me, and it felt like I was living and feeling these moments as well. I wish there were more poems in this collection. It was an absolute delight.

– Judge 76, 27th Annual Writer's Digest
Self-Published Book Awards

Made in the USA
Monee, IL
14 April 2022

HEIGHTSARTS

Date
W, 26, 22

First Name
ED

Last Name
RyBKA

Phone
(216) 851 0038

Email
EwRyBKA@gmail.com
EwRyBKASS@gmail.com

Street Address
13715 ShakuBlvd #2B

City
Cle

State

Zip
44120

Mailing Address (if different from above)

City

State

Zip

OVER

I am interested in more information on (please check all that apply)

___ Music Programs   ___ Public Art   ___ Exhibitions   ___ Poetry

___ Membership   ___ Volunteer Opportunities   ___ Other _____

I ___ am ___ am not a donor   I ___ am ___ am not a member

Is this the first time you have visited Heights Arts? ___ Yes ___ No

If so, how did you hear about us? (or other comments)

_____